FLIP-FLOPS & FALAFEL

A handy guide to Morocco in a motorhome

by

Andy Mckettrick

A big thank you for all the support

and encouragement during the writing of this book.

"No-one will ever buy it"

"I harbour all the same worries as most
The temptations to leave or to give up the ghost
I wrestle with an outlook on life
That shifts between darkness and shadowy light
I struggle with words for fear that they'll hear
But Orpheus sleeps on his back still dead to the world"

Thanks David, for always being there

Andy

Introduction

Okay, so we've all been there. You've got the van full of baked beans and curry, the missus has packed her knitting and you have a route planned out for the winter away.
Boxing day, south towards Dover. A day or two to travel through France (too expensive) before entering Northern Spain.
Head slowly down the coast then February and March along the Costa del Sol. Spend April in the Portugese Algarve before heading back to the UK for May. It's a good plan. Thousands of people do it.

Slight problem though...

Most of Yorkshire and every old fart in a bungalow have decided that their lives would be so much better if we were all limited to just 90 days in the EU in every 180.
The fines system is already in place for Third country (Non-EU) nationals overstaying in the Schengen area and they are in the region of 700 euros for a 48 hour overstay.

But don't worry. We have spent the last decade of winters in Morocco. It is a brilliant place for motorhomes.
In this book, through experience, I'll attempt to tell you everything you need to know about travelling in a motorhome in Morocco.

A month in Spain, two or three months in Morocco then a month or so to make your way back slowly to the UK. Easy.
You can still go back home in May. Sod their 90 day rule!

Table of Contents

About the Author

Born in Anfield , Liverpool in 1966.

Best Travel writer 2019 for 'Beer, Baba & Brexit'.
Featured four times in the New York Bestsellers list.
Currently based in L.A with his long term life partner Fred.

Other Books By Andy Mckettrick

Beer, Baba & Brexit

Learn the guitar in just 39,000 easy steps

The Clangers

Coronation Street – Behind the glamour

Pride & Prejudice 2

Manchester United – Surviving relegation

Chapter 0. A list of useful Arabic or Berber phrases.

Salam – Hello

Lebes – How are you?

Waka – OK

Salam malecon – May peace be with you.

Ana smīti... – My name is...

Ana Men...... – I'm from......

Shokran – Thanks

La Shokran – No thanks

Afak – Please

B'shhal? – How much is this?

B'slema – Goodbye

B'seha – Enjoy your meal/snack/drink

Yddek fi Zob – Listen Officer, you're getting on my tits now so go and hassle someone else! (Only to be used as a last resort and if you fancy a night or two in a cell)

Chapter 1. Africa...Is that in Europe?

Morocco is a gorgeous country full of amazing friendly people but remember, it is Africa not Europe.
It is not Tenerife or Magaluf. Don't come expecting Happy Hour, a full English breakfast, a pint for a euro and a Chinese on the way back to the van. This is NOT Mini-England.

You'll see dogs. Lots of stray sunbathing dogs and cats. Both harmless. You'll see plenty of litter, along the floor, in the bushes, and on the dogs. You'll see midgets with no teeth. If you've ever driven through Manchester then none of this will be new to you.

When you tell your family and friends that you are going to Morocco, you will get the usual "Please be careful. The world is a dangerous place" and my personal favourite "Isn't it full of Muslims and close to Iran?". FFS.
If any of them bothered to put down their Daily Mail and spend 5 minutes on Google they would see for themselves that travelling in a motorhome in Morocco is a far safer option than Europe.
For example, during the last decade there have been two terrorist attacks in Morocco but sixty four in Europe during the same period.
Don't get me wrong. They all mean well in their own 'Alf Garnett' way but when was the last time a family member told you to be careful when visiting The Lake District?
There were 650 murders in the UK during 2019. Nearly 150 of them in London alone, yet I don't recall getting the "Please stay safe" Facebook message as I drove past Dartford!

So, ignore them.
In fact, tell THEM to be careful while you are away.

You'll be fine.

Chapter 2. Before you go

The process of entering Morocco has simplified a lot over the years and now all Customs ask for when you disembark the ferry is your passport, your vehicle Log book and a Green card.

We normally get our Green card from our Insurer, Comfort. If your Insurer wont issue you with a Green card for Morocco then cover can easily be bought from one of the booths as you disembark the ferry in Tangier Med. It costs around £72 for the month.

We always buy our ferry tickets from Carlos at Viajes Normandi in Algeciras. It costs 180 euros for an open return and comes with free wine and a cake! (Actually, this time it was Cider and biscuits)

If you prefer, (or if the missus is nagging you) you can buy your tickets online in advance but it will normally be more expensive.

Over the years we have tried the crossing via various routes but prefer the Algecias – Tanger Med option.
Tanger Med is a new, modern port and is less of an 'experience' than getting off directly in Tanger town, for example.
This year though, we had a two hour queue to get out of the port at Tanger Med. The customs officers are so slow. I've seen quicker Man Utd defenders!

Tip – Never cross on a Saturday lunchtime. We've never had a problem during the week. Also don't be afraid of taking a late crossing. You can sleep in the port when you arrive at Tanger Med, without any problem and then start fresh the next morning.

At Viajes Normandi they will exchange some Euros for Moroccan Dirhams for you plus there is a Currency booth as you exit customs in Tangier Med that offers good rates and with no comission.

At the moment (Feb 2020) you get around 12.5 Dirhams to the pound. You can also withdraw Dirhams direct from any Bank cash machine but this normally comes with a 3 euro fee.
There are banks in virtually every town that you pass through.

There is no need to arrive with thousands of Pounds or Euros.
By far the best method is to use a cash machine and just draw as many Dirhams as you think you'll need that week or for the fortnight ahead.

We normally just draw out 2000 Dirhams. This lasts us a good few weeks in Morocco, including diesel, food shopping and eating out.

Chapter 3. The Dog.

For the last 6 years, bringing our dog, Gordi, to Morocco couldn't have been any easier.
We just made sure his Rabies injection and worms treatment were up to date and his passport had the relevant stamps.

"Fancy popping over to France next month, love?"

"Ooh, that'd be great. Let's go"

NOT ANYMORE, I'M AFRAID.

Now, thanks to Leave voters, you will now need to have all your dog's paperwork and vaccinations up to date and in order at least 4 months before you plan to leave the UK and enter Europe.
No more spur of the moment trips. Lots of planning ahead.

Apparently, along with the extra '£350 million' per week now being poured into the NHS this is also one of the benefits of leaving the EU!

All the up to date information on travelling abroad with your pets can be found on https://www.petguard.co.uk/brexit-pet-travel

Most villages in Morocco have a number of stray dogs lying around but don't worry they are quite harmless.
If they get too close for comfort just pick up a stone and look like you're going to throw it and they'll run away.

Giving the little stray puppies the odd handful of dog biscuits sounds like a great idea but just bear in mind that they will then sleep underneath your van all night and be waiting for you outside your door, the second you wake up!

Please, please, please, before driving away, check underneath your van for dogs.

This year a French couple packed away their things, said their goodbyes, started their engine and promptly ran over a little puppy.

"Aww, at least it was over quick", I hear you saying.

Well, nope. The poor thing crawled out from under their van, its spine crushed to pieces. Screaming in pain, it pulled itself across the sand dunes towards the mother, using just its front legs.

We just stared, helpless, crying.

Anyway, the French couple took it to the nearest vet in Tiznit, where I'm glad and sorry to say, it was put out of its misery.
So, again, please just check underneath before driving away.

A flea collar or shampoo would be a good thing to bring because apart from the Moroccan village dogs, you will come across quite of few of those French full-timers. You know the type. They live in huge removal lorries with massive dogs.

Everyone's got dreadlocks and they love shite techno music!
An extra flea collar for yourself could come in handy if you get too close to them :)

Chapter 4. Go to the shops!

A list of items you may consider buying before crossing over to Morocco. Mainly because they are a lot cheaper in Spain.

Wet wipes – For when you're low on water :)

Toilet paper

Toiletries

Dog food – Their favourite will be hard to find

Olive oil

Decent cheese

Nice crackers or Ryvitas

Good tea bags

Good Instant coffee

Pork products with a long expiry date. eg...Bacon, Chorizo etc...

Lots of Alcohol. It is possible to find alcohol in Morocco but may require a long drive to a Carrefour. In Agadir you will find alcohol for sale in most cafes and restaurants, especially along the promenade. A cold beer will set you back around £1.60 a bottle. Not too bad if you're gagging for a bevvy!

Chapter 5. What stuff costs

Fruit & Vegetables - Potatoes, Carrots, Oranges, Courgettes etc...cost around 40p per kilo. Spanish grown, imported fruit like Kiwis cost a lot more, obviously.

Diesel – Costs around 80p per litre.
Afriquia seems to be the cheapest chain of stations. You can also fill up your water tank at these stations for free or a couple of Dirhams. If you keep your eyes open as you drive around Morocco you will see fresh water taps in most villages.

Butane gas – Large 22 kilo bottle costs less than £4.
They use the French style adapter/regulator which can be bought for around £2 in any hardware type shop. One bottle lasts us about 3 weeks for the fridge, cooking and showers.

If it's your first visit and you don't have an empty bottle to exchange then they will expect a deposit of around a tenner on the bottle.

Tip – Ignore the scare stories about the gas in Morocco. Our fridge/freezer has worked perfectly for the last 10 winters, although I admit that sometimes it can smell different to what you're used to.

Drinking water – From 75p to 90p for a 5 litre bottle from any shop.

Fresh bread – 10p to 15p per loaf depending on how white your face is and whether or not you're wearing socks with your sandals.

Fresh cakes – From 10p to 50p each. Always ask the price first or next minute they'll be a quid :)

Fizzy drinks – In a cafe, Fanta & Coke are about half of the price you'd pay in the UK.

Chicken/Beef/Vegetable Tagine = We pay around 30dh (£2.70) for a single person tagine or 50 to 60dh for a larger one for two people to share. In really touristy places like Agadir, you will pay a lot more.

Milk – 10dh per litre (Quite expensive at 90p)

Minced Beef – Around 80dh per kilo (£7)

Chicken/Turkey breast – around 60dh per kilo (£5.50)

Fresh eggs – 1dh each (8p)

Four chocolate biscuits – 1dh (8p). Dentist filling – Around £20

Cheese and butter – Around the same price as in the UK

Windscreen wiper covers – 50dh each (£4.40)

Campsites – from £4 to £10 per night

Good fake Converse trainees – 100dh (Around £8)

Baboushas (Hand made leather shoes) -100dh

Yogurts – 2dh each

Floor mats for outside the van – Around 150dh m2

Re-upholster all chairs and sofas in van – Around £300

Fake Adidas/Nike T-shirts – 100dh (Around £8)

Spices – If you love to cook then you'll find a great selection of spices in Morocco. We found them cheapest in the large Marjane supermarkets but you can buy them in all the cities.
Our favourite is Ras El Hanout, which is a mixture of six ground spices: Ginger, White Pepper, Coriander, Turmeric, Allspice, and Cinnamon.

Successful Negotiation Tactics when shopping

Walk away (or at least pretend to begin to walk away).

Have an amount in mind that you are willing to spend.

Counter offer with a price that is about half of their initial asking price.

Don't buy from anyone rude or aggressive.

Have fun!

Every shop owner will give you some spiel about anything you pick up. "This is good quality camel leather" or "this is handmade". Don't believe everything you hear. You'll need to do a thorough check yourself!

Chapter 6. T'Internet

Sorting yourself out with internet in Morocco is so easy.

Maroc Telecom stores and Pay as you go sim cards are easily found in any decent size town, like Asilah, Larache, Essaouira etc...
Cost = 80p per gigabyte of data. (10dh per gigabyte)

You just need to show your passport and in 2 minutes you'll be handed a shiny new sim card which you can use every year. We've been using the same one now for 4 or 5 years.

Pop it into any mobile phone and use it as a hotspot or use it in one of those handy little Mi-fi routers.

Simple to top up with more credit.

Go to any little convenience store and ask for "Maroc Telecom Recharge" and then say how much you want...eg 10 Dirham 20 Dirham or 50 Dirham.

You can even buy a 20gb recharge card which should last anyone a month!

A 2gb/20 Dirham recharge card

Scratch off the back of the little card they give you and send a
text with the long number followed by *3 to 555.
Easy. You now have Internet in the van.

Tip – Bring your tablet or Firestick. Netflix & Amazon Prime work
a treat.
Also, download an Android app called BeeTV from Google play.
It's free and a great app for watching Movies & Series if you have
enough data. We've been using it for a couple of years now
without any problems.

Chapter 7. Wildcamping

Don't be scared to 'Wildcamp'.

We very rarely use campsites in Morocco. Maybe only 2 or 3 nights during our 3 months stay.

Another option is 'Guarded parking'.
Most places you stop at will have a little toothless man in a Hi-vis jacket who'll tell you it's between 10 – 40dh to spend the night among other motorhomes.

Quite a lot of people seem to feel safer in large groups of vans but personally, we prefer the free, smaller, hidden places on our own or with just 2 or 3 'neighbours'.

Most campsites allow you to 'empty and refill' for a couple of quid plus you can quite easily empty your cassette at a petrol station toilet, if really desperate.

PLEASE DON'T GO ALL 'FRENCH' AND EMPTY YOUR CASSETTE IN A BUSH!

Morocco is very safe but as in all countries there is theft and petty crime, so use the usual common sense regarding locking up properly, putting valuable items out of view and not walking around with 3 grand in your wallet, is recommended.

We often leave our table and chairs out all day and overnight without a problem. We simply chain them to the van if we're going for a long walk along the beach or into town.

Our favourite 'wildcamping' spot in Tafraout

Chapter 8. Getting around

Toll roads - Morocco has a modern system of toll motorways.

It costs around £30 to go from Tanger all the way south to Agadir.

They don't accept cards on the motorways so make sure you have some Dirhams before you leave the port.

Tip - Don't play Scrabble with the locals!

You'll never win!

N roads - There is also a great system of free N roads that you can use to get around.

R roads – Regional roads that tend to be quite good.

Any roads smaller than this can be a bit hit and miss and quite bumpy.

Taxis - There are three types. Grande, Petite & Horse taxis.

The Grande (usually a Mercedes) taxis charge only 5dh per seat and go out of town, for instance, from Tiznit to Aglou beach. They'll charge a set fee to go to the airport, for example but you can ask for the 'counter' to be on if you prefer.

The Petite taxis charge 5dh per seat but only go to destinations within the town or city.

The horse taxis charge 5dh per seat but only go up and down the same street.

Tip – With all taxis, bear in mind that unless you pay the 5dh for every seat in the car, you will end up sharing the vehicle with anyone who gets in along the route.
I jumped in a Mercedes taxi one time and said "Hospital". By the time I arrived there were 8 of us all squashed in together.

Buses - Buses also charge 5dh per seat within the city limit. They are operated by ALSA, the same as in Spain but sometimes, out of the towns, the bus stop can be a bush or a tree! Just look for where everyone else is waiting.

So you've decided to take a road trip in Morocco but you've heard driving on Moroccan roads is a nightmare.
Driving around Morocco in a motorhome is the best way to travel.

Here's all you need to know about driving in Morocco, with some helpful advice about how to approach the few things you're unfamiliar with.

~

The minimum age to drive is 18 and you should always carry your driving license with you.

European citizens don't need an International Driving Permit for Morocco. Check before you travel in case this changes post Brexit.

Moroccans drive on the right and give way to traffic from the left. (unless they're on a motorbike or a donkey, coming towards you the wrong way)

Morocco has no drink drive laws but they do have alcohol laws. Get caught drinking and driving and you can expect the police to throw you in jail. Don't drink and drive.

Road signs are almost identical to those in Europe.

Driver etiquette isn't something they're familiar with in Morocco. Moroccan drivers don't give way to pedestrians and often park on crossings. You don't have to copy!

As a rule of thumb, the speed limits (unless there is a sign indicating something different) are:

60 km per hour in urban areas
100 km per hour outside urban areas
120 km per hour on highways

Morocco's traffic police can issue on the spot fines for breaking these speed limits, so drive sensibly. Getting pulled over for any traffic violation is likely to ruin your day.

Roundabouts - There's no consistency when it comes to the give way rules of a Moroccan roundabout. The official rule is to give way to traffic already on it but it's not always the case.

At some, drivers already on the roundabout will all stop to allow you to enter. At others, drivers seem to follow the official rules. The locals appear to know what rules apply to which roundabouts. We've never been able to figure it out so just assume you need to give way. Regardless of whether you're joining the roundabout or already driving on it, prepare to stop.

Animals - Donkeys pulling carts are a common sight in Moroccan towns and cities. More often than not they will ride on the right edge of the road and you'll need to take care overtaking of course.

Night time driving in Morocco - We have little experience of this because our number 1 road trip rule is we don't drive at night.

Chapter 9. Keeping yourself busy

As we all know, spending months on end together in a small confined space can sometimes get a bit stressful.
To avoid the temptation to strangle each other, it's important to keep yourselves busy. Below are the type of things we do to amuse ourselves on our travels when we are not out exploring.

Buy a Fitbit bracelet. Walk at least 15km per day.

Paint. Try to do a watercolour of wherever you are.

Learn to play the guitar (This is soooo difficult).

Always go for a coffee and watch the world go by. Making one in the van just isn't the same!

Do jobs on the van that you've never had time to do.

Write a blog/book/diary of your travels.

Shop daily for fresh produce. It's an experience.

Mingle with other campers (Maybe not the French or Cockneys)

Have Card nights.

Learn a language. Duolingo is a great free app.

Avoid any UK news. Who gives a f**k?

A few of our efforts

Chapter 10. Plantlife.

Ladies, put down your knitting. It's time to look at some plants!

Each Spring, the Anti-Atlas Mountains and meadows are cloaked with a colourful array of beautiful flowers.

The region is also home to the indigenous Argan tree, Argania spinosa.

A selection of springtime flowers

Purplius lavendus

Whitius bushius

Greenius spikius   *Littlius onitsonius*

Petalius enormius

Seriously, I have very little interest in plants and flowers but the Anti-Atlas region in the spring has some amazing wild flowers and you can get some great photos.

Tip – Bring your good camera.

Chapter 11. Hiking in the Anti-Atlas Tafraout region.

WARNING

Trekking and scrambling can be a dangerous activity carrying a risk of personal injury or death.
The author cannot accept any responsibility for any loss, injury or inconvenience by any person using this book.
So, if you fall and break your arm in 23 places or a wild boar chews your left leg off, don't come running to me for compensation.

Route 1 - The Elephant's trunk.

From the main group of motorhomes, head right until you find the blue markings on the floor. Follow these until you reach the base of the Elephants Trunk. Scramble your way up the left hand side of the hill until you first see the rock circles below then take a sharp right and head up to the ruins of the house that sits on the summit.

Worth doing for the views of Tafraout alone!

Retrace your steps back down to the bottom. Don't be tempted to find a quicker route down. There are some big drops.

Time 2 hours from the vans and back.

Level - Easy Peasy.

Approaching The Elephant's trunk

Amazing views from above

Route 2 - Napoleon's Hat.

Head out of Tafraout on the R107 passing Maison Troc.

After 4km you'll arrive at the small village of Aguerd Oudad.

Find the mosque and head to the top of the main square where a set of stairs begin. After the stairs, Zig-zag your way up the hill passing old ruined walls until you cannot get any higher. At this point you have two options. You can squeeze through the skinny gap, hoping nothing moves and kills you or you can chicken out, like a girly Southerner, make your way down and head back to town for pizza, telling everyone that you reached the summit. :)

Time – 1.40hrs   Level – Easy

"Okay. I'm coming, You small B**tard!"

It can get quite tight!

Route 3 - The painted rocks.

From the main group of vans, walk past Camping Tazka and through the palm trees and French vans towards the actual town of Tazka. Carry on past the mosque and the blind, screaming Berber woman (have a dirham ready. She's like a troll) and out of the village. After about 10 minutes, keeping to the left, follow the green dots on the rocks and make your way up the slight hill.

Once at the top it's a flat, extremely warm, 40 min stroll to the start of the painted rocks. There's no water tap at the site anymore so take enough for the whole walk.

Time - 2 hours return. Very easy but can get very hot so start immediately after breakfast.

Route 4 - Samson's peak.

Walk through the main group of vans towards the highest hill around. It's obvious which one because it's has two upright slabs of rock on top which you can stand between for your own Samson photo.

Keep to the left walking up until about 10 minutes from the top, it changes to a scramble, using your hands to reach the summit.

Time - 2 hours return.

Relatively easy apart from last tricky 10 minutes.

Take a picnic. The views are the best around.

Getting the 'Selfie' photograph between the two slabs can be quite tricky.

Take care not to drop your mobile phone or camera.

You'll never see it again!

Route 5 - The surf board.

Starting in Tazka, with the entrance to the Mosque behind you, if you look directly ahead you should see a pylon at the bottom of the hill. Work your way anti-clockwise around the private property until you arrive at that pylon. From there, scramble your way up the hill. Normally you can follow a trail of little stones left by previous climbers.

After about 30 minutes, you should arrive at a large tunnel-like opening to your right. After making your way through this, the Surfboard rock will be directly in front of you.

Time – 1.5hrs return. Level – Hands needed.

The Surfboard

Route 6 - The valley of the Lion (with optional sneaky beer and feet in the Auberge pool).

Walk through the main group of motorhomes and out towards Samson's peak. Follow the route up to the right, passing the boulder with the hole in.

Zig-zag your way down the other side, following the paint markings or little rock piles until you reach the bottom.

Carry on following the newly cemented route markers until you reach the entrance to 'Auberge Chez Amaliya'.

After a lovely rest you have two choices...back the way you came or follow the road for around 50 mins until you reach the entrance to Tafraout. Ice cream time!!!

Time - 5 hours.

Level - Quite easy but tiring if it's hot. Check the weather.

Gallery

Horseriding – 200dh for the hour along Taghazout beach

Two Slapheads!

6am over Marrakech

Napolean's hat soaring above the little town of Aguerd-Oudad.

Tifnite & The painted rocks near Tafraout

"C'mon you reds"

Sunset at Sidi Kaouki

After spending 300€ on the van

It can get quite hot, inland in March

The gang in Tafraout

"Jump"

"5dh? I'll give you 4"

"Stop laughing and HELP!"

Chapter 12. Places to visit

Travelling in a motorhome we tend to avoid large cities, for obvious reasons. Below, in no particular order, is a list of places we would recommend to visit.

Asilah   35.474156, -6.027209

Great introduction to Morocco. Old Portuguese colonial town.
Nice Medina (old walled centre) and the usual crazy street full of
shops where you can buy anything you want. 40dh per night to
park directly facing the sea or cheap but basic campsite for
around 60dh.
Large crumpets from the old Berber woman outside the Medina
gates. 1dh each. Mmmmmm.

Good opportunity to try your first hot bowl of Moroccan soup
(Harira). Costs between 7 – 10dh.

Nice stop for a night or two and a little taste of what's to come!

Plage Sidi Boulfdail   29.704093, -9.951961

We absolutely love this place. Peaceful and totally free!
About 14km or so south of Aglou plage. Amazing beach parking.
Take the right turn directly after Club Evasion holiday park.
There's a water tap in the actual village and the Luxury surf
complex 'Greenwave' will let you empty your cassette for a few
euros.
Must be one of the best beaches in Morocco! There's one little
shop in the village. Try the traditional homemade bread. It's
delicious! Whilst in that shop, the owner will ask you if you know
Amelia Earhart. He will then proceed to show you a folder full of
photos of Amelia and detailed plans of her plane. Next minute
he'll whip out an old piece of metal and tell you that it belonged to
her plane and his grandfather watched her crash into the sea
directly facing his shop. "Would you like to go out and see the
wreckage of her plane?" he then asks. "I can take you out on a
boat". All sounded fascinating and I really fancied doing it but the
problem is Amelia crashed and died over the Pacific!

Plage Sidi Boulfdail

Agadir

Large beach resort with all the usual all-inclusive hotels you find anywhere in the world.

Difficult to wildcamp and the campsite in the city centre is horrible.

Better to stay in Atlantica parc camping (**30.587723, -9.751389**), fifteen miles away and visit the city whenever you fancy.

There's a large choice of restaurants along the promenade and a huge Souk open every day except Monday.

Tip - Visit 'La Medina de Agadir' and 'The memory museum' about the terrible earthquake in 1960 that killed 15,000 people.

Agadir & The Mother in law.

So, the mother in law decided that she needed a weeks holiday in Morocco, a week before her next holiday in Mallorca, only three weeks after a holiday in Tenerife and a just a month since her last holiday in Mallorca!

This woman spends less time at home than Judith Charmers!

Such a shame that she's one of those Daily Mail readers that support ending freedom of movement, so now they're getting the 90 day limit in the EU. That's fair, I reckon.

They also voted to scrap the EHIC health cards for Brits that they've always used for their holidays. Genius!

Never mind, I'm sure private health cover for anyone with existing medical conditions should only cost around 3 or 4 grand a year!

My Mission (if I chose to accept it) - Find a suitable 4 star hotel in Morocco for 3 people for less than £30 per night. A pitch black bedroom, a comfy bed and a fridge big enough for all the alcohol and chocolate!

Plus we need to be able to park the van safely and visit everything of interest in walks no more than 50 metres long.

Tricky, you're thinking!

Problem solved.

Hotel Ocean Atlantic. £200 for a 3 bed apartment for the week.

Only minutes to the beach and a score of 8.6 on Booking.com.

Hotel Ocean Atlantic pool area

Can't believe we said goodbye to our free spot on the most gorgeous beach in Morocco to go and stay in a concrete block in Agadir but I bit my lip and it was over soon enough.

To be fair the hotel was brilliant, we had a good week and it was nice to have loooong showers.

The staff were amazing and our van was parked right in front of the reception security cameras. Sorted! :)

La Medina de Agadir

Now I'm sure that we've all heard the classic "Those Muslims should respect our customs if they come to the UK. This is a Christian country with Christian values"

Sounds great, doesn't it except for the fact these are the very same people sat outside KFC on Agadir promenade in Morocco, topless in a pair of trunks and flip flops! Practice what you preach, Kn**heads!

Tip - Remember Morocco has a small minority of Christians and Jews but is mainly a Sunni Muslim country so try to respect their customs whilst visiting and cover up slightly more than normal when walking around towns and villages.

L'Oualidia   32.731974, -9.043336

Safe parking among at least fifty other motorhomes.
Lovely view over the lagoon and a gorgeous long beach.
Guarded parking for 30dh per night with toilet emptying facilities
and free water for your tank.

Great boat ride on the lagoon. 40dh per person.
You may even get it cheaper if you're a better haggler than me!
The town has everything you need. Saturday souk (market)
Plenty of shops for your fresh fruit and vegetables.

In my opinion, the best Beef & Vegetable Tagine in Morocco is
sold here. Fifty dirham for two people. Best between 1-1.30pm at
the restaurant with the blue chairs, Pepsi umbrella and the
butchers at the back. Mmm!

Tafrout   29.714838, -8.986270

Our favourite place.

Tip – Don't arrive before Valentines day. Too cold at night!

Pay 15dh per night to the guardians in the palmeraie .
They patrol all night with their torches.
Water van comes every day and charges 25dh to fill your tank
and any empty bottles that you may have.
You can have your rug out, awning out, washing out.
No-one cares. Feels very safe. We love it.

Great walks to the Painted Rocks, The surfboard and The Lions
face etc...

New french style 'Borne' service area at the entrance to the
village next to the mosque. 10Dh for 10 minutes of fresh water.

Good selection of cafes, shops and a weekly Wednesday souk.
Great salads and pizzas at Hotel Espace Tifawine.
Best Moroccan soup at Cafe Tagadirt – 7.5 dh.
Grab a nice coffee and decent wi-fi at Hotel Salama.

For us, this is Morocco at its best. The village is big enough to keep you entertained for a few weeks. There is every type of shop you could ever need including food, clothes, mechanics, barbers etc...

The locals are accustomed to tourists and are extremely friendly without wanting anything from you in return.

If we could only visit one place in Morocco, it would be Tafraout!

The scenery is unbelievable.

The Almond festival and strolling through the valley. Brilliant.

If you fancy an excursion in a 4x4 or need to rent mountain bikes to go exploring, then Saíd from Maison Touareg is your man.

He's a great source of information about the Tafraout area and has a good selection of Trekking/climbing books and maps that he will gladly let you borrow.

Saíd is a genuinely friendly man and has a great selection of Moroccan rugs, clothing and jewellery in his shop.

Hassan, over at Maison Troc also has a good variety of rugs, berber jewellery and furniture etc...
He has rooms to rent too, just in case your family fancy a visit!

Our little Gordi hates his guts though, so we try to hide when he passes us on his moped! Not so easy because Hassan seems to be in every street, in every minute of every day!

Not to be missed – La Kasbah Traditionnelle in Tazka and the nearby village of Oumesnat with its Berber houses and ruins.

LA KASBAH TRADITIONNELLE
—— T A Z K A ——
MUSÉE

MAHFOUD IDHIHI
GÉRANT

0673.82.90.54

f FB/KASBAHTAZKA
TAZKAHOUSE@GMAIL.COM
VILLAGE TAZKA TAFRAOUT, TIZNIT - MAROC

Mahfoud, a local Berber man is the owner of the Kasbah.
The house has been in his family for 16 generations, over 600
years.

He's slowly restored it over the last 20 years to its original state.
You'll get a guided tour, all in good English then into the living
room for Moroccan tea and biscuits.

The view over the valley from the roof terrace is amazing and
from summer 2020 there will be a lovely Berber room available to
rent in the Kasbah.

The visit only costs a couple of euros and is highly
recommended.

The village of Ousmenat, only a five minute drive from Tafraout, offers a chance to explore the traditional architecture of an old house in the Ameln valley that has been standing for no less than five centuries! **Tip** – Park outside the village near the mosque.

Mirleft   29.590237, -10.036832

Guarded parking for 12 vans overlooking one of the cleanest
beaches in Morocco. 20dh per night. Good little town too. Weekly
souk on a Monday. Great little street in the centre of town that's
like something from a Western movie.
Locals swear that Jimi Hendrix was here.
Breakfast with coffee, cake & orange juice for only 13dh on the
roof of Restaurant Cherouk.

Tip - Fill up your water tank at the Lavage (car wash) place
directly facing the petrol station. 10dh.

The parking at Mirleft Plage

My barber in Mirleft (let's call him Youssef) told me that his King is a bad man. "Morocco people are homeless with no food and he's rich" he said. "Your Queen is different. She's nice! English nice. No racists"

I didn't want to ruin his day so I just nodded and never mentioned Pervy Prince Andrew, the 2,300 foodbanks, The Daily Mail and the fact that in 2020 around 51% of the UK would quite happily stab Youssef in the face and throw him back into The Channel without a seconds thought.

Aglou plage   29.804422, -9.832707

Decent campsite Camping Aglou plage (70dh), if needed and good parking facing the promenade that has half a dozen cafes.

Only 20dh to the guardian for an overnight stop in front of Hotel Aglou Beach.

Free Wi-Fi that reaches the vans from the Hotel and you can easily empty your cassette in the public toilets directly opposite for only 2dh.

Along the beach, you can walk either way for a few hours especially when the tide is out.

Tip – Nice coffee and cake at Cafe Idou Aglou, on the promenade.

"Forty dirham each bracelet" the jewellery man on the prom said. Lucky enough, they love beer more than they love Allah, so 4 cans of cheap Lidl beer later, I walked away with 4 bracelets.

Total spent = 84 cents. Result!

The cheapest jewellery in the world!

Tip - From the parking at Aglou beach you can jump in a taxi or bus straight to Tiznit.
Both options cost only 5dh per seat.
Tiznit is a great town for shopping.

Legzhira beach   29.443456, -10.116654

Free parking and overnight without any problem above what's probably the most famous beach in Morocco.

In the past there were five huge arches along the length of the beach but a few have collapsed over the last decade so only one or two remain. Still impressive, though.

No services but half a dozen cafes and quad rental available. (150dh per hour)

Great stopover for a night or 2 on the way to Sidi Ifni.

Sidi ifni   29.383194, -10.175830

Old Spanish colonial town that was still Spanish up until 1969. Because of that it feels slightly different than most places. Quite a few campsites to choose from ranging from 70dh upwards. Lots of cafes and restaurants and a weekly souk.

Although Arabic is spoken among the younger generations in Sidi Ifni, the older generation speaks perfect Spanish.

The Iberian spirit still lingers on. People still have a 'siesta' and many of them still prefer to speak Spanish over English. Then there are the many Art Deco buildings and the street signs that could be in Madrid or Sevilla.

Tip – Try the chicken curry at Restaurant Nomad. Nice!

The Art Deco Town hall

Sidi kaouki   31.349215, -9.794295

Nice long beach with half a dozen restaurants. Couple of cheap, basic campsites if you're in need of services etc...Tip - Don't hang your washing out on the metal clothes line in the campsites. You'll end up with more holes in your clothes than a kid from Salford!

Met Hippies Luke and Orthelia. They are travelling the world in a tiny tent. No money. Friendly couple.
Tip - If you ever meet them and Orthelia invites you to share their raw chickpea tagine with them, simply say you're leaving for Spain that afternoon. If you have to, leave for Spain that afternoon. Anything to avoid her cooking!

Great wild camping spot on the cliffs overlooking the beach, 5km south of the campsites. A really friendly soldier comes to chat and checks your passport. Total calm.

The secluded beach just south of the town. Bliss!

Serious question – Only one in ten people are left-handed/footed. So how come three quarters of all abandoned shoes are for the left foot?

Bit of Advice for 'Lefties' out there.

If you leave the house wearing two items of footwear, simply look down and check that you are wearing two items of footwear before returning home. It's not that difficult!

Imsouane   30.841845, -9.820557

Parking along the 'prom'. 10dh per night.
You will only get told to leave in the evening if the campsite
complains. We have stayed for 3 or 4 days without any problem.

Full of rich white twenty-somethings carrying surfboards.
Slightly more expensive in the cafes (due to the surfers).

Nice hippy feel to the town. Great walks along the cliffs.

Tip - Great coffee with a view at Cafe Momo.

Chefchaouen   35.165901,-5.262070

The city was founded in 1471 in the Rif mountains by Jews and Moors fleeing Spain. I heard a lot of different (some quite unbelievable) theories about why Chefchaouen is blue.

Some say it was painted blue by the Jews who settled there after fleeing Hitler, others say it's to keep the mosquitos away, while some just said it represents the colour of the sea.

I'm not sure which version is true, but it seems to have worked out well for Chefchaouen, as it sure looks good in blue!

There's one campsite that's overpriced at nine euros but there is a car park where you can stay overnight. (co-ords above).

Chefchaouen is one of the most touristy places you'll visit in Morocco so two days there would definitely be enough.

Taroudant   30.464592,-8.878647

Taroudant is a former capital of Morocco, built as a base to attack the Portuguese on the Atlantic Coast. The city walls, which are almost completely intact, were built in 1528.

The city is sometimes called 'Little Marrakesh'. There are two souks either side of the main square. Both great for shopping.

The impressive city walls

Guarded parking along the walls

The motorhome parking is along the walls and costs 50dh per night.
If you fancy a campsite then I recommend Camping du Jardin at **30.476942, -8.843664** which costs 60dh for the van & two people per night. They make a good tagine too!

Tip – Eat at Restaurant Jnan Soussia, a great little place.
The surroundings are beautiful and the chicken kebab, fab!

Sitting out, resting from all the walking and having a beer when it occurred to me that women have been fooling us for decades.

"Eat brown bread. Don't forget your muesli. C'mon, finish your yogurt"

Well, I've just noticed on the back of my can of lovely beer 'Calories 98. Fat 0g. Sugar 0.1g'.

The yogurt I had for breakfast had 102 calories,3g of fat and 1.2g of sugar. So F**K yogurt. Drink beer! Otherwise you will end up with a 'yogurt belly'.

Taghazout   30.545716, -9.712019

Surfing village with a 'Hippie' vibe just north of Agadir.

Lots of privileged little white kids walking around topless, wearing woolly hats in 26°. Good massage parlour down the side street to the fishing port. Ask for the 'lucky finger'. Your life will never be the same again :)
The town has changed a lot over the last five years and lost some of it's charm but still worth a visit.
Wildcamping was stopped in this area a few years back but recently vans have been creeping back around the town.

Tip - Go for the famous Half pizza/Half salad at Le Spot. 50dh.

'Chilling' in Taghazout

Paradise Valley   30.588236, -9.531959

Gorgeous pic-nic spot where you can swim or watch the crazy
Moroccans jump in from the high cliffs. We've never tried sleeping
but paid 10dh for guarded parking during the day. There are two
cafes in the valley if you fancy a tea, coffee or juice.
Tip – Don't go too early in the morning. It's cold!

Tifnite plage   30.193909, -9.637850

Typical Moroccan fishing village just south of Agadir.
Overnight now tolerated if you park near the military post.
Nice beach walk. A few 'cafes' and a gorgeous trail through the
sand dunes. Free. We like Free.

Tiznit   29.692841, -9.726762

Good town for shopping for all your supplies with a decent campsite (Ryad Camping) a mile or two outside on the road towards Tafraoute.

We ordered 2 fresh chicken breasts at one of the local chicken stalls. "Five minute"he said then promptly turned around, grabbed a chicken by its neck and swiftly chopped it's little head off before I could scream "Forget it, we'll go to McDonalds".

Great, clean dentists here if needed. 25% of the cost of a UK dentist.

Tip - New windscreen wipers will be offered to you by a couple of young lads. Don't go above 100dh and they'll cave in eventually!

Essaouira   31.511705, -9.764937

In Arabic, Essaouira means "Little picture" and literally,
Essaouira is a little picture. A small, breezy town with a long, wide
beach.
Essaouira is a great place to take things slow, whether that
involves an afternoon of peaceful walking or pottering around the
numerous shops that sell spices, painted bowls, rugs and
Moroccan clothing. The town has a lovely 60's 'Hippie' feel to it.
The Medina here is the perfect place to stroll round, hassle free.
Great long beach and good overnight parking directly outside the
Medina walls. The guard will ask for 50dh but we always just
laugh and offer him between 20-30dh to sleep for the night.
Don't cave in. It always works

Tip – Eat at La Petit Perle. They do a great 3 course lunch for
only 75dh.

"Eh Abdul, you've ordered the sign too big!"

"Don't worry. I've got an idea!"

Meknes   33.890690, -5.564220

Meknes is one of the four Imperial cities of Morocco. It's known for its imperial past, with remnants including Bab Mansour, a huge gate with arches and mosaic tiling. The gate leads into the former imperial city.
The motorhome parking is directly outside the Medina entrance and costs 50dh to overnight. It felt safe and is relatively quiet.

We enjoyed this city. Its maybe the prettiest in Morocco and isn't too difficult getting in and out.

Tip – Visit the Medina, El Hadim square and Bab Mansour gate. Great Beef & chicken Tagines at Restaurant Gout de Meknes.

Meknes is in the Top 10 cities to visit in the world in 2019 according to the The Lonely Planet tourist guide.

Chapter 13. Meals on wheels

In Morocco, with fresh food being so cheap to buy, we eat a mountain of vegetables every week. Below are a few of the meals we make using only one pan.

Lentils

Simply put anything you fancy in a pot with some pre-soaked lentils (spuds, carrots, onions, whatever), bring to the boil, simmer for 30 mins then add a stock cube and a bit of salt & pepper before serving.
Best eaten with a Moroccan baguette costing 10p!

Chicken & Chickpea stew

This one's really tasty.

Throw chicken, onion, peppers, chickpeas, chorizo, garlic, a stock cube and spuds in the pressure cooker or large pan.
Bring to boil then simmer for half an hour. Gorgeous!

As with all our recipes...best eaten with a nice baguette!

Vegetable stew

Place a load of fresh vegetables of your choice in the pressure cooker or pan with a stock cube and cook for 30 mins.
Once cooked, season to taste then run out to the nearest village for a kebab or pizza, leaving the missus to eat it alone!

Ergh! This recipe's mainly for women or men that watch cricket.

Spanish Baked rice

My favourite van meal but you'll need a proper British van with a gas oven and not one of those silly European models with 3 rings and a 40w microwave!

Lightly fry whatever meat your fancy in a Pyrex dish over a low flame. Chorizo, Black pudding, sausages, whatever.
Add a few cloves of garlic, a stock cube, one cup of round rice, 1 sliced potato, slices of tomato and two cups of water.
Throw it in the oven for 30 mins on gas mark 7.

Again, eat with a baguette and a nice glass of red.

MMM!

Fabada (Spanish Bean Stew)

Another one of my favourites. Fry some onion and garlic in a large pan or pressure cooker. Add chorizo and black pudding. Throw in the pre-soaked beans, a stock cube, cover with water and cook for 30 mins. Season to taste.

Tip – Keep the quilt tight around your neck at night!

Scouse with Mince beef

Another tasty and very easy to make classic.

Fry an onion, chopped garlic and beef mince for 5 or 10 mins then add the potatoes, carrots, peas, a beef stock cube, a splash of Lea & Perrins and water. Bring to the boil and simmer for 30 mins. Season to taste and serve with a nice bread bun.

Tip – Women tend to be tempted to add all kinds of healthy S**T to this recipe eg celery, courgette etc...DONT. It's perfect as it is.

Epilogue

Little did we know what would happen to turn our world upside down at the beginning of March 2020.

Whilst sat in Tafraout, Covid-19 spread around the world infecting over 200,000 people every month, killing thousands every day. We contacted the UK ambassador to Morocco, Tom Reilly, via email and Twitter.
"Get yourself to Ceuta or we cannot help you", he responded. We didn't sleep much that night. It would mean a 16 hour drive. Over 1200km in just 24 hours.

"OR WE CANNOT HELP YOU".
I couldn't get his words out of my head. We took his advice.
We had to leave.

We packed up and left Tafraout to head north towards Agadir. Only stopping for coffee, nearly a whole day later we arrived at the Moroccan border with Ceuta. Knackered. We turned around the last bend and...OOF! 1000 vans. Over 4km of them. The Spanish authorities in Ceuta had closed the border to everyone.

This is where it's starts to get funny (unless you were one of us in that queue).

That afternoon, UK ambassador tweeted **"The border is now closed. Go back to where you came from"**. WTF. The queue was patrolled by Moroccan soldiers and police. No-one was allowed to leave. Road blocks were in place now to stop any movement between all Moroccan cities.

After a long 3 days in that queue, watching the French empty their cassettes on the beach and without a single reply to any of our messages from the UK embassy, we finally received the tweet we'd all been hoping for.

"To all those stranded in the queue outside Cueta. Don't worry. WE ARE GOING TO GET YOU OUT!" Tom. UK ambassador.

The next morning he tweeted "Thanks to the French ambassador and the Moroccan authorities, Tanger med will be opening it's car park to the campervans until we find a solution. There is water, showers, toilets and electricity"

Suddenly and without any choice, at 8pm, in the pitch black, we were guided by the military for the 16km drive over the mountain and down into the vast port parking area.

Stalag Luft III

The Moroccan military took everyone's details as we entered.
"Passports" he demanded.
"Err...hang on. Is this where we can stay until the border reopens?" I asked.
"Until we find a solution" he replied.
"If we don't like it are we free to leave" I responded.
"No, but you have everything you need in here. Water. Food. Everything"

Not convinced and with the wife crying in my ear, I told them to let me turn around and get out of the queue.

"OK, if you don't like it we will give you authorisation to travel somewhere else" the soldier confirmed.
Stressed and tired I caved in and we drove in towards the British section.

We awoke the following morning to realise that we were in a massive car park surrounded in all sides by motorway.
"Let's have a look around, find where everything is" the wife suggested.

Noooooo! There were over 1000 of us in there. Mainly French.

No showers. No electricity. Four toilets and four water taps. The Moroccans were positioning a portacabin which later would act as a shop.
I charged up to one of the soldiers guarding the entrance.
"I'm not staying here" I yelled "I want permission to leave"
"Later. Later" he replied, dismissively.

Back in the van I urgently messaged the UK ambassador.
"Can you tell us what medical advice you took before herding us into a car park with over a thousand people, all sharing four taps and four toilets?"

I attached a photo of the toilet/tap area. Within 5 minutes I was blocked. The UK ambassador to Morocco, Mr Tom Reilly had blocked me on twitter! Ian and Sue in the van alongside had been blocked also.

Suddenly, the reality of our situation sank in. We were prisoners. Abandoned by the only person that could help us.

The facilities for 1000 'prisoners'

Day 2.

"We have no money to buy anything. No food. Can I go to the bank?" I asked the Colonel Gaddafi lookalike at the gate.
"No" he replied. "Later, Later". This was to become the standard reply to any question.

Time for action. We were on our own. No-one was going to help. The escape committee was formed.
Work initially started on three tunnels codenamed 'Tom', 'Dick' and 'Harry'. Cunning methods had to be devised to remove the soil from the tunnels without getting caught, so we would shake the dirt out of our trousers and onto our flip-flops at various points around the compound.
Although the three tunnel entrances were finished by Tuesday afternoon, work on 'Harry' and 'Dick' stopped at 4pm so that efforts could concentrate on 'Tom'.

Day 3.

Wednesday morning. 'Tom' was discovered by the guards :(

That afternoon in March 2020, work on 'Harry' resumed. By 7.24pm, the 500ft long tunnel was ready.

That moonless night, 10 British, 2 Kiwis, 2 yanks and a couple of Scousers climbed out of the escape shaft, shored up by the bedboards from Fat Simon's Hymer.

Disaster. Due to a miscalculation, the tunnel was a few feet short and we came up on the wrong side of Ken & Lynda's 15 year old Concorde, leaving us with a heart-stopping dash back to our vans. All that effort for nothing. Denise lost two nails, Ken, an Apple gadget and we haven't seen Gordi's flea collar for days.

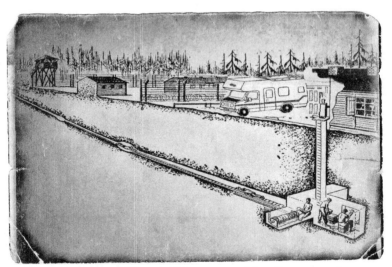

The map of 'Tom'. Discovered by the guards

Oops!

Day 4.

A crowd started forming around one of the French vans. On it's roof were the French and German ambassadors.
"A boat will be coming to liberate you. It is a commercial boat and the tickets for 2 people will cost around 1450€. You have no other option. Your existing ferry tickets are not valid."

We told the German ambassador that we had been blocked from contacting the UK ambassador and he stared at me in disbelief. "If you can't afford the ticket, borrow the money. Camper vans have been barred from travelling on the roads. You cannot stay"

Day 5.

We mostly moaned about the French.

Day 6.

A Moroccan turned up at the compound. He told us that he was the 'honorary' consul to the UK embassy (meaning, the day before, he was selling oranges from the back of a pick-up).
"Where is Tom Reilly, our ambassador" I asked.
"You need to understand that this is an emergency situation and stop asking me questions" he replied.
Eh? WTF. No questions allowed. Great!
He was about as much use as forward gears in a French tank!

Day 7.

Faced with no other option and worried about what would happen to us if we didn't get on the ferry we reluctantly handed over our bank details and our 1500 euros.
The German ambassador turned up later and handed out the ferry tickets to the Germans. He passed by our vans and asked us if we were OK. In all honesty, we weren't. We were upset.

Why was a German checking up on our welfare? Why wasn't Tom Reilly here handing out our tickets?

He had advised us to come to this compound. Announced to all the world that he was 'getting us out' then stopped all contact. Washed his hands of us. To the world, he made himself look like our saviour. In reality any help or advice we received came from Jorg, the German ambassador.

To be honest, we were not that surprised.

We watched the chaos in the UK as the woefully underfunded NHS struggled to cope with the virus without any protection.

We saw Boris the clown waste £5.8 million on sending letters to the nation telling them to stay at home when he could have just as easily announced it on TV.

We witnessed first hand how the French and German embassies in Morocco acted swiftly to calm and help their citizens in trouble and how the UK ambassador couldn't even be bothered to turn up.

Between us we joked that Tom Reilly was probably sat in Cheshire somewhere on his mobile but really it wasn't funny. It was negligence. Simple.

Day 8.

14°. Pissing down. Still waiting for the boat.

Day 9.

Finally, there was movement. A police convoy took us all directly to the port. Five hours too early! Temperatures taken. Vans sprayed with disinfectant and we were allowed to board for our two day voyage, in the wrong direction, to the South of France. Jorg, the German ambassador stayed on the dock to make sure everything ran smoothly.

"Goodbye and good luck" he said as we made our way up the ramp onto the most overpriced 'rescue' ferry in history.

Where the F**K was Tom Reilly?

*None of the above is in any way a criticism of the Moroccan authorities. They were brilliant as always and looked after us as best they could in the circumstances. The British Embassy, on the other hand, was a different story!

See if you have better luck than us at finding Reilly :)

I hope you have found this book helpful. If so, I'd be very grateful if you could leave a positive review on Amazon.

Happy travels

Andy

Notes

Printed in Great Britain
by Amazon

11868705R00078